Pimps, Pastors, Pulpits and Prostitutes

THE NAKED TRUTH

Bishop Woodrow H. Dawkins, Jr.

Order this book online at www.trafford.com
or email orders@trafford.com

Most Trafford titles are also available at major online book retailers.

Printed in the United States of America.

ISBN: 978-1-4669-2959-3 (sc)
ISBN: 978-1-4669-2957-9 (hc)
ISBN: 978-1-4669-2958-6 (e)

Library of Congress Control Number: 2012909908

Trafford rev. 06/12/2012

 www.trafford.com

North America & international
toll-free: 1 888 232 4444 (USA & Canada)
phone: 250 383 6864 ♦ fax: 812 355 4082

My name is Bishop Woodrow Hayes Dawkins Jr. I am writing this book because it moves me to sadness to see some of the things going on in some of our churches today. In addition, I am titling the book *Pimps, Pastors, Pulpits, and Prostitutes.*

Let's start with the pimps. In some of our churches this day and time, some of our pimps are the pastors. Yes, that's right, the pastor. Let's first see and find out what it does take to be a real pimp today. I am at this time in my fifties of age. I have lived to see many things go on in many of our churches. In my lifetime some were very good and some not so good, but in the last times, the Bible tells us that many things would happen.

Well, getting back to defining a pimp, a pimp is a person who knows how to manipulate a woman's or a man's mind/brain in order to get them to do what they want them to do. Such example is some of the pastors in the churches today. Some will use power over the people to get them to beckoning their every call, even going as far as sleeping with them. I know this to be true for some pastors that I know. Not only do they sleep with the unmarried men and women in the church, but some of them will also sleep with the men and women who are married as well.

Persons who are weak in mind and weak in spirit, those are the kinds of people that the pimps will go after. They're called vulnerable people. Some of the pimps in the church have gone to college and learned how to brainwash the people in order to rob them of their money but don't stop their go on their body and, at the end, all their self-esteem, and when they finish with that one—meaning, when you have nothing more to give to him—they move on to the next weak one. The pimp is always looking for a new body and mind to add under his or her power. To control, the pimp will find the weak person and convince them that they are on their side and they care about their welfare, but what the pimp really wants is to have you get everything for him/her; the pimp would have you think that he or she is doing this because they love you and understand you when no one else does. This is called manipulating the mind; it goes on all the time in churches all over the world, and it has happened to me as well before.

Previously we have some very smooth-talking pimps in the pulpit. They are called pastors. If you are not careful, that pastor that's pimping God's people from the pulpit will try to pimp your man or woman.

Let me tell you how to spot a pimp in the pulpit. When you see a pastor closer to your woman or man than he is to you and he or she will do what that pastor told/asked them over what you say, that's a smooth pimp that has too much power over your man or woman, and you will see or can look out for things going wrong in your relationship down the road. Anytime a woman is closer to the pastor than she is to her husband, then something is wrong, and the same goes for a man to the woman pastor. The good leader will not be a pimp and will not try to take advantage of the people/members but will do as the Lord tell them. God is not going to tell you as a leader to go and have sex with the sisters in the church. That's part of why we must not just drop our guards to the pastors. This is not a beat-up time on the pastor, but it's time for the church to be the true church of God and for true men and women of God to stand up and do what God has called them to do. The first thing we must do is to spot the pimps in the pulpit and who are pimping God's people from the pulpit and then get them out. But before we can move toward doing that, we must want the pimps out. Remember, after the pimps brainwash the prostitutes/misuse God's people, not all want to be made free; some want to stay a slave to the pimp even when you try to save them because the pimp has convinced the prostitutes that he or she is the best thing for them. This is the way it is in many of our churches. There are women and men that are under a spell of the pimp/pastor that would, if could, leave their mates for the pastors, and some have and are still doing this now all over the world.

I know of some pastors that ended up leaving their wife for a church member. It doesn't stop at that. If a pimp/pastor would misuse his or her power to pimp the man or woman in the church, then what will stop them from using it on the children of the church and in the homes of the members and others? That's the power of the pimps. As I stated before, some preachers go to school/seminars to learn how to use mind control over people. I call that pimp school, for some of our churches have turned the church over to the world to run. It was a day when we had real godly men running the church. Where are they now? Now we have pimps running the house of God. What many of the pastors/pimps want is for the members to go out and bring in the money to them; isn't that what the pimps in the streets do? In addition, the pimp in the street thinks that all the money belongs to him/her; then they give to the prostitutes whatever they want to, if anything at all is given. Is not things working the same way in the church? You go out, bring in the money/people into the church, and the pastor reaps from it. Do you have a pastor that goes out with you to get the people, or does he or she tell you it's your job? Pimping is going on and you are being prostituted and don't even know it.

The same thing had happened to me as well. God never told us to go get people and take them to our building in order for them to be hurt by the pimps in the pulpit called pastors. Think about the people that told the other people to go with them to church and how the pastor slept with the woman that you brought to the church and how it broke up her home. We do not need to take people to a building in order to take them to Christ. First of all we must take them to the Lord, not to our pastor. If you take a weak person to a pimp, what do you think is going to happen to that person? The pimp's goal for the person is to use them until they use them up.

I have more respect for the pimp in the street than the pastor that hides behind the robe and the pulpits. Don't misunderstand. I don't go along with either one. They're wrong. What I am saying is when you go to the pimp in the street, you know whom you are going to, but when you go to church, you do not expect to run into the pimp in the pulpit with a robe on, but what you do hope to find is a loving, godly leader that cares for your souls, not someone that can't wait to take advantage of you. That's what I meant when I said that I had more respect for the pimp on the street than the pimp/pastor in the pulpit pimping God's people from the pulpit. Both are wrong. Pastors/men and women in power have taken and are still taking advantage of weaker people/members in the church. Sisters should not be with a pastor alone. The same goes for a man and a woman pastor. In addition, some of the things that are going on could not happen.

I guess you may by now have asked yourself why I am writing this book and why I would say the things that I am saying. First, I did not take pleasure in writing these things. In other words, it hurts me to hear so much about my brothers and clergy in the gospel. Yes, I did say clergy in the gospel. I am a preacher of the gospel of Jesus Christ for over thirty years, and this book is true. Some of you that read this book can relate to some of the things in this book. I have had the chance to talk to some pimps from the streets. Some of the things that I was told did not surprise me. I had my time in the street, and I saw how things work in the street. Also I got the chance to see firsthand how they work in the church. I was raised in a little, small Baptist church. This book is in no way about that church or any one church, nor is it about condemning any church. It is written in order to open the eyes of the reader and to help heal those who have and are still being pimped out by pastors in your church. Stop letting it go on any longer and being exposed to this practice and put a stop to it. This is the same as the pimp in the street and also a form of a cult-minded person or, better yet, a Pharaoh's way of thinking pimps/pastors prostituting God's people from the pulpit.

The Lord is telling you to let his people go in order that they may serve the Lord, not you. Let me tell you how you can tell when you have a pimp in your pulpit. Sometimes you will hear them say "my people." When Jesus called Peter to himself, he said to Peter, "Feed my sheep." I did not know that we as pastors had any people of our own. The pimps in the street think they own people too. This is the mind-set of the pimps. This is why the church is in the condition that it is in now. Man wants to rule over God. Jesus said if he be lifted up, he will draw all men to himself, not if you or me. We now have men going to school to learn how to preach and talk about money. Boy, if the church that they end up in does not have enough money for them, then they are going to move on to the next one. I want you to stop reading for a moment and think about how far we have gone, yes, gone, not come. The church has gone so far away from God until we just don't know how to get back. The leaders have failed the people/members. We think more is better. Once again that's the way the world thinks. At what price are you willing to pay to keep pimping out yourself, kids, and all that you know in order to get what you want and in the end you will lose it all? Because when the pimp finishes with you, he will kick you to the curb. Some pastors will play members against one another and favor one over the other.

Look at the pimp. They do the same things. The pimp in the pulpit and the pimp in the street are the same. The pimps have the same aim: to get all and what they can get from you no matter what, whatever the thing is that they want from you. If you would look back on your life, then you will see some pimps that you had come into contact with that tried to use you in some way in the street or in the church.

I remember a pastor. I went to his church to preach one Sunday, and this particular day, I was led to preach about how men try to have power over the people and make people think that they are some powerful man or woman, and this pastor/pimp would do things to get the members to run to see what the pastor wanted. I just sat and looked on. This was done two or three times. I said to myself, "Lord, how am I going to preach this message today after seeing this display?" I wanted to change the message so bad, but I could not change it. Sometimes God will give you a word that if you could, you would change it, but what we need are more preachers that are sent by God and not made by man.

I don't think it's wrong to go to a seminary school, but if you are going so you can make money off the back of hardworking people in the church, then you are just like the pimps in the street. I do not think that many pastors know what the true responsibilities of the pastors and leaders are to the church. Someone got it wrong; the responsibility of the leader/pastors is to lead the church as Jesus did. He did not pimp the people's bodies, gifts, or anything else that they had, and this is the way our leaders should be today. We leaders must go back to understanding we are the servants of the most high God and the way we serve is to serve God's people without charge. You work for the Lord, not for the people, but when you turn it around, then you become a pimp in the pulpit and call yourself a pastor that prostitute God's people, and when the pastor goes to tell the church how much the church is going to pay them, that's the same way the pimps in the streets do. Also the street pimp will tell the prostitutes how much money they better bring to them. The church will do the same things in its own way. Once again you can see the pastors in the pulpit are operating just like the pimps in the street do.

Here is another way to spot the pimp in the pulpit: they are going to always talk about how to put money in his/her pocket through and by the way of the church. When was the last time the pastor talked to the church about the church members getting a blessing from the church? Something to think about, isn't it? Is anything wrong with you getting blessed by the pastor? The pimp in the street is always telling the prostitutes in the streets that they are going to buy them something. Why can't you share in the harvest? If you share in the labor, the Lord will let us share with him. He said if we suffer with him, then we shall reign with him. It sounds like to me that's a cool pimp in the pulpit pimping the people.

I have been working on this book for many years; at times I didn't know if I would write it or not. I have asked myself, what will people think about it, or would anyone even care to hear what's going on in many of our churches today, or do they know and turn a blind eye to it? And early one morning, I awoke, jumped out of my bed, ran to my computer, and began to write. I have always wanted to write a book, and there were times when I would start and stop, but today is the right time to write.

I'm reminded of another story that happened. It was in this church where the pastor attempted to rape this young lady, but it was stopped and he was taken care of and dealt with, but just think about all the cases that are not talked about, like the women that did not tell her husband or her boyfriend or her father and her uncle because of the power of the pastor, deacon, or just a church member who told you not to say anything to anyone.

Here is another way to spot a pimp in the pulpit: when he/she tells you whom to talk with and whom not to talk with, the reason for this is if you hang out with strong people, then you will become strong and they can't get to you like they want to. Wives, stay close to your husbands. Children, stay close to your parents. The people in the church are too trusting with the pastors. Why would I say this? And even if I am a preacher, I say this because it's the truth. Look around at the things that are going on in and out of the church today, but when you are looking, please keep in mind that the things that you see did not just start happening in the churches. It's been going on for a long time. You had your eyes closed or your back turned, or you were part of it. You choose. Do you remember when that pastor went over to you and put his or her arm around you and hugged you so tight till it was hard for you to catch some air? Now you know that your husband's father or your boyfriend or your girlfriend doesn't give you long, tight hugs like that. Some men and women will go to the church just to date and meet. Don't you know that's what some of the pimps/pastors do? Also the Bible tells us that in the last days, there will be many false prophets, false teachers. Where do you think they will be? In our church, in the pulpits, pimping and prostituting God's people, and some of the people will be just like the ones on the street. They will like it and will not want to change. It's the same way in the churches now. The pimps are already in the pulpit and are at work, and the members have heaped unto themselves, and we wonder why our children are acting the way that they do. Some of the children have been trying to tell some of you for a long time that something was wrong, but you would not pay them any attention until it was too late. The pimp had you brainwashed, and about the news that you have heard on TV, about the pimps in the pulpit that were said to have had sex with some boys in the church or outside the church, it doesn't matter where it was; it should not have happened at all.

Once again I would like to say for the record, I am in no way beating my brother, but what I am saying is that we put too much trust in the pastors. God has warned us about putting trust in man, saved or unsaved. In addition, it is not just the pastors that you need to beware of; it's some of the deacons of the church. There are some cool pimp deacons in some churches also. I have heard about some of the deacons, and I know some things firsthand.

Let me tell you a little bit about this one pimp/pastor that can tell you a lie faster than you can blink your eyes ten times. At a time I was in need of a car, but I did not ask anyone for a car or any money to buy a car. I heard a knock at my door. I went to answer the door, and who was it at my door? It was this preacher that I know. I said hello to him, and he spoke back. I asked him to come in. He did go in and sat down, but before we got started into a deep conversation, he said to me, "Let me tell you what God told me to do for you." Keep in mind what I told you, the reader: I did not ask for anything from anyone. The pastor said to me, "God told me to go buy you a car and give the keys to you." I asked him, "Are you sure?" He replied yes. I said, "Thank God," and then told him thanks. That had been over eight years ago, but that's not all. He came to me a second time before the eight years was up and told me the same thing. I looked at him and wondered about him. I thought to myself, was he trying to convince me to believe what he was saying, or was he trying to convince himself? In addition, years later he had the nerve to ask me to start up a church with him. I will only build on the truth or not at all. A truth teller and a liar can't work together, light and dark don't go together, preachers and pimps should not be sharing the same pulpit. The pastors in the churches should not be pimping God's people from the pulpit.

I can't help but think about this one time when I was in this particular city at this certain church. I was in the pastor/pimp's study, and as we were talking, the pastor started talking about women's body parts. I'm going to let you use your imagination on what parts he was talking about, but as he was talking, I was thinking to myself where did all these thoughts come from, who did this pastor think he was, and who did he think he was talking to.

Once again, this is some of what we have in our pulpits, but this also is what some of us want in our pulpits, and we will defend it if part of the church speaks out against the reason we want this type of pastor, which is because we are trained to go along with it. Just like the prostitute in the street, the pimps have trained them like some of the pimps in the church have trained some of the people in the church as well, but that's not all. Don't you know that you have some pimps in the pulpit that have in the church a wife and one or more girlfriends and the church members know about it? However, that is not the sad part of it. The members will sit under it and justify it with "We all have done wrong" and "It is not I. It is he or she." In addition, with that same way of thinking, we can sit back and let the pimps in the pulpit pimp out our sons and our daughters.

This takes me to another story, there was this one pimp/pastor that would work the people in the church and not pay them. You know that's not right. It was not right doing slavery and it's not right now. Once again that's a pimp in the pulpit. The pimps in the pulpit do not care of the age; they want what they want. It is the same way with the pimps in the street: they want what they want, not thinking of the age.

Moving right along takes us to this next situation. We also have some pastors/pimps in the pulpits that don't work along. They have some of the men in the church, running what is called interference. For them they help the pastors cover up/hide their wrongdoings. It works the same way with the women pastors who are doing wrong too. Wrong is wrong and right is right. Until we give the church back to God and let him give us our leaders, then will we keep picking leaders after our own hearts, not leaders after God's heart. The flesh is flesh and the spirit is spirit.

That's not to say that the one that God will send you won't ever stumble or even fall, but what I am saying is that the one that the Lord will send will have a heart for God's people, and that, my friend, makes all the difference in the world. The pimps/pastor preaching from the pulpits do not have your best interest at heart, nor do the pimps in the street. I know as you read this book, for many of you it brings back thoughts and memories of the past that you had suppressed and you are saying to yourself, "How does this man know about me?" In addition, who told it because I didn't? Well, you are not alone; there are many like you out there that have some very bad experiences with a pimp in the pulpit that did you wrong and you had no one to talk to. This is now your voice. This book will uncover and reveal the lies. For those that can relate to some of the things that you are reading, I hope you will find some relief or total healing from the things that you have endured at the hands of the pastor/pimps preaching from the pulpit. Because we still have many of pimps/pastors in the pulpit at this time, they are in it for the money, the house, the car, the women, the men, the fame, and a way to get to your kids and for all the wrong reasons. You know this to be the truth. There are some that will read this book and say why a preacher would write a book like this. If the preachers won't tell the truth, then who will? That is what is wrong with our churches today, and that is why we have so many pimps in the pulpit today. It is because the church of old, where the true pastors would care about the people's souls, is gone, but now some in our churches are pimps in the pulpit. In addition, the list goes on if the church did a survey and the whole church would tell the truth of how many people in our church have and are still having sex with the pastor. I wonder how many people would tell the truth and ask the pastor how many people he/she would like to be with. Keep in mind, the pastor is married. The Bible tells us not to lie to one another. I can tell you what most would say: that's none of anyone's business, but God and I wonder, would anybody answer the survey? Would you answer?

The Bible says, "Know them that labored among you." How much should we know? And some of us don't want to know. This is how the pimps get into the pulpits. We don't know how to pick the right people for the job. Most of us will never pick Jesus to be Lord over our life and to tell the truth about things. We will go along with the way things have always been run. But keep this one thing in mind: if you do the same thing, then you will get the same things; if you change, then things must change. If the pimps in the pulpits do not move, then you move. Let me ask you this: if a bear comes into your home, are you going to tell it to depart from your home, or are you going to leave? Some of you will say, "This is the church that I've always attended," "My mother and father went here," "This is where I will die." That just may be true. That's what the pastor/pimp is banking on: that no matter what he/she does, you will always support them even in the wrong that they do. That's what the prostitutes do also. If this is the way that you think, then you just proved that this book is to help you break free from that way of thinking. The pimps on the street will beat the women and do much more, and they will not leave them, and we will ask the question, why won't they run away? Why won't they run away from the pimps in the pulpits? Something to think about: why when the women that work in the church and doing the will of the Lord have to worry about the pastor trying to go with her and hit on her, trying to sexually assault her at the church or at her home, and why, when she called the pastor to go to her home to pray for her because she is sick, he tried to have sex with her. Some pastors have gotten some of the women in the church pregnant, and they have a wife in the same church, and they want the wife to support him in that that's a pimp in the pulpit and will tell the wife to get over it. And we have some of the deacons that are sleeping with some of the pastors' wives.

Why am I telling this? If you pull the cover off things, then you can see what's in the bed and then you can make a better judgment of what you want or need to do. If the reader of this book would have read this before they made some of the moves that they made, then they wouldn't have done some of the things they did. But this book can still help you make better diction in the future. When you go to your next church, watch that deacon, the pastor, and the teaching and look out for that smooth-talking voice. But, above all, watch out for the power that they want over your life because if you go to a church that has so much going on all the time from Sunday to Sunday and you don't have time for your husband, your children, your wife, or yourself and the only one you have time for is the pastor, then you have come across a pimp/pastor in the pulpit. Let me tell you what you must do. Hear me real good. Run away as fast as you can and do not look back. Do not answer the calls from that pimp/pastor.

Let me tell you about another one of them that I came across in my thirty years of preaching the gospel. I myself had to learn how to spot them. This is one way to spot some of them: they will sit back and tell you what to do but they will not do anything themselves. That's what pimps do. Even down to doing what the Bible says, they will tell you how to live, but they won't do it. Now don't get me wrong. The Word of God says, "For all have sinned and come short of the glory of God," but also keep this in mind. It says that we have that. Do not say that we are to live in it but to live free of it. And the church has so many pastors that do not know the true Word of God; they are not teaching the truth to the people. You can't teach something that you do not know. This is why many of our people end up in some of the things that they do: because they have not been told the truth and some do not want the truth. If someone went to you and told you that they are willing to teach you the Word of God free, do you not know only very few people would ever take that preacher up on his offer but they will gladly pay a pimp/pastor to pimp them out? That's something to think about. Jesus gave this same offer for years, and so did I. Over thirty years I have preached in many of churches and seen many of things go on that God had nothing to do with.

Some of our leaders try to put the Lord's name in things that He had nothing to do with, when we should just come clean and tell the truth. This is what I am trying to show you: that some of the smoothest pimps are in the churches' pulpits today and that's why our church is upside down. We have been pimped out like prostitutes and do not even know it.

Let me tell you of another pastor that pulled off a big theft. It was this other preacher that loaned this other pastor some church equipment. It was in value over $2,000 or more. The pastor was just a nice man, and he took a chance trusting the pastor. He soon learned a high-price experience. Some of the preachers are the biggest liars. He never got back the church equipment, but he did get a good lesson from that smooth-talking, so-called pastor. I wonder, what will that pastor do with the things that were taken though theft and lies? I think about pastors that have done this kind of thing. And I would ask myself, how can they sit in church and use it as if they paid for it? How can you preach to the people from the pulpit about not being a thief and all the time you are the one using stolen church equipment to run the church of God? And did the members know that many pastors are doing just this?

It is 3:00 AM and I am up writing this book. There is such a pressure on me to write this book. I never had one this strong before. I just could not sleep; I had to write. In addition, as I lay in my bed thinking about the pastor that pimps God's people from the pulpit, I could not help but wonder what went wrong. I said to myself, "What happened to them? How has a good pastor turned bad?" I also asked myself, "Did the people turn them by letting them get away with so much wrongness in the church, or was that pastor a pimp from the start?" I think this is what happens to some of the pastors that turn into a pimp pastor. When that pastor starts off as a pastor, he/she starts off right, and as the membership grows and the money grows, so does the temptation. That's like a pastor that has a storefront church with a few members in that church. Everything is okay, but as the Lord blesses that pastor to grow to have many members in that big church, know that the thinking of that pastor changes. You are now looking at the bigness of God, not yourself. You are the same size as before. God is the big one. This is the mind-set of many of our leaders/pastors today: when you move from the little storefront church with the membership of a few and then you have the membership of many people and you forget where you come from, then you become a pimp pastor because you think that the people are yours, not God's people, and you start treating them like they are your property. That's what the pimps will do with the prostitutes in the street; they also think that the women belong to them.

Sometimes, good pastors turn bad, and that's when a pastor becomes a pimp in the pulpit. You do not have ownership of people; only God does because He said all souls belong to Him. So I only have this to say to all the pastors out there: let's work hard to change the wrong that we do into right. In addition, the pastors should start back working with one another and stop being territorial. That's what the pimps do in the street; they think that certain blocks belong to them and the women belong to them. Once again I need to remind you that the people do not belong to you but they belong to the Lord and only to him. And one more thing that can change a pastor into a pimp pastor is the spirit of greed. See, that spirit has no end to it.

I have had the chance to witness many pastors get that spirit in them and could not shake it off. That greed spirit will turn you to do anything to get what you want. You will lie, steal, cheat, hurt the ones that you said that you love. I have seen where some pastors make it big, as some would call it, and when they do and when asked to go speak to a small group of people, that pastor would turn that group down, and what is this that has happened to our pastors that if you do not have a certain amount of money, they will not go to your church and preach the gospel to you? I am so glad that Jesus did not do this to the world. Is that a pastor that would tell you such a thing, or is that a pimp pastor pimping God's people from the pulpit? You tell me. I myself have preached the gospel for over thirty years and have never told anyone what to give me for coming to preach the gospel to them, and never will I, the Lord told me, to go without charge. I am not trying to make myself more than any other pastor or preacher, but what I am saying is this if the Lord said "Go without charge," then why are most of the pastors charging? Let's take a closer look at things. Now we do know the pimp sends the prostitute out to make money, and after that they make the money; then in return the prostitute will come back and pay the pimps for pimping them on the street, so is this what is going on in our churches today? Is the church paying the pimp/pastor for pimping them out but we just use a different name for it but it's still the same?

Not only that, also I am reminded of another thing that comes to mind when I was much younger. It was this older lady. She would go to church very often until she got so sick that she could no longer go. But after she stopped going, I noticed that the church members did not go by very often to see how she was doing, but I would only see them when it was time for her to get her check. I would talk with her, and I asked her a question. I asked her, "Why did the pastor only come to your home after you got your money?" She told me that he would come and pick up her tithes and her offerings. That really stuck with me as a young man, and I asked myself, how can a pastor do this to a little old lady? But as I grew up and was called to the ministry, I have seen so much wrong done by men who were called pastors that made me not want to be in that bunch with them, but the Lord had to deal with me about what I saw. The spirit told me why I had seen what I saw. It was that I would not go that way. I had preached for twenty-plus years before I would let anyone give me any money/love offerings. I saw pimps in the pulpit as a young boy, and all throughout my ministry, I can only thank God that I am the way that I am, but I always pray for my sisters and my brothers in the gospel, but I just can't help but think about them not getting the big church or the sum of money. If they did then, would things be different? Well, it's a lot of ifs, but we can say this: it is what it is, so we now must deal with it. The pimp is in the pulpit; what do we do?

One thing I do know that we must do about it is pray and do what the Lord says do Let's take a good, hard look at the TV pulpit. We cannot forget about some of them as well. There are some pimps in that pulpit. What about when the pastor is always asking for your money to stay on the air, some of the things that are preached are not true, and if that pastor will not preach the whole truth and not pick out what they want to say, then I say come down because you cannot get people saved if you will not tell them the truth, because the Bible says you shall know the truth and the truth shall make you free. If you want to free the people by telling them the truth, then you must want them to stay bound. That's the same thing that the pimps want with the prostitute; he/she doesn't want them free because they are making money off them.

We have some pimps in the pulpit on the TV. In addition, the way to stop that pimp is to stop the money flow, and if you want to find out if you have a Pastor or a pimp in your pulpit, just tell them that you all are not going to pay the pastors, and see what they will say, but tell them that the church members are going to bless them out of their bosom as the Lord leads them. I will not tell you to do what I won't do, but a pimp will tell you to do what they won't do. If you have a pastor that will tell you to do something that they won't do, then you have for yourself a pimp pastor.

Let's take a closer look at another thing that bothers me about the pimp pastors. Have you noticed how some of them are able to have planes and fine big homes, nice cars, and the finest things in life? There's nothing wrong with that if they worked hard on a job for it, but if it's not from an outside job, let's take a closer look at you, the members. Maybe not you (but you), the one that can't pay your bills, and the pastor is telling you about the story in the Bible that said this woman had a little meal and oil. She made some food with what she had, gave it to the man of God to eat, and how the Lord blessed her. That story is true. The man of God blessed her by him being a man of God, not by being a pimp. The Bible talks about you being blessed by blessing one of God's people, not by blessing a pimp in the pulpits who is prostituting God's people. The question is, to you, how does it look for you to pay my light bill and the next day your electricity gets cut off? Is the pastor going to let you and your family stay with him? Or better yet, you and your family are walking but you are making the payment on his nice car; is that what Jesus did to the people? For me, the pastor's job is to make sure that the members are in the same state of living or are better than myself. The pastors are the servants, not the members. This is why the church is upside down, and I am trying to turn it back right side up. I know that it is a big job, but someone needs to do it, but first I must let the people know that they have for a long time been fooled by the pimps in the pulpits. Now after I sound the trumpet/cry aloud, show the people what's going on, it's all up to the reader. I hope this book will help many to see more clearly about where we have come from and where we are, also how we got here and where we go from here. For God is not happy with what is going on in the church today. Let's pray for our brothers and sisters that have been overtaken by a fault, for we are to restore them. In addition, do not forget the ones that they have wronged; pray for that family.

In addition, I cannot help but think about all the people that will go home under a bridge to sleep at night and the pastors that have these big churches and big bank accounts will go home to a fine meal with the family at night. Have you ever wondered why we have so many churches and things are not getting any better? Well, let me tell you something; one of the reasons is that we have the wrong leaders in the set leading us out of all the churches. This country should not have one homeless person sleeping under a bridge, but sleeping in a bed like you and I do. The pimps in the pulpits need to stop robbing the people in and out of the church. If the pastors of all the churches would be led by the spirit of God and not by greed, they could come together, sit down, put a plan together, and buy up these emptied buildings, convert them into houses for the homeless people and help find jobs for them; but it is too much for some of us to do because it's too much like right, we would want to know who these people will be and who will get the money if and when they would make any. That is what pimps want to know as well.

The church has become so out of focus that it cannot even see God. We as a church have lost what we had as the leader of the world, the light, has almost gone out. It's time to put this oil in your lamp before it is too late. As a people of God, I am pleading you to come back to the fellowship that you had, if any, with the Lord. Let him save or renew you. We all have done wrong and at times need to be renewed. Even David, a man after God's own heart, had to asked God to clean and wash him. There's no shame in asking the Lord to help you to get back right with him, but the shame is when we won't ask him. Remember, that pride cometh before the fall. It is a sad thing when a pastor thinks he or she is better than the members of the church and they don't need forgiveness too. That's the pimp way of thinking. They do not see it to be wrong in what they do, and the pimps in the pulpit think the same way too. The people that go to a church and sometimes take their family go to hear the Word of the Lord that will help them. They did not go to be hurt by the pastors or the members.

There are so many people that I run into that give me some stories that make me want to cry. I sometimes find myself telling them that I am so sorry. I know that I am not the one that did the things to them, but I am a preacher too, and I will ask them not to hold what happen to them with one pastor against all preachers. The world does have some good ones. Some of the pastors that have gone with some of the sisters in the church and had children are not taking care of them and do not want anyone to know about it. You need to step up to the plate and take care of your responsibility. There is no reason to run away now. The time when you should have run, you didn't run, so do not run away. Take care of your children like you should. If you lay down, it is now time for you to stand up, and some of our pastors have told the women that they had gotten with children to abort the baby, and that is what some of the pimps will tell the prostitutes to do when they have children. That's something the Lord will deal with. Oh, by the way, I think of the people in the church playing a part in the pimps in the pulpit. Think about it, if you will. There was a time when we trusted God's Word more than we did the pastor's word because the pastor's word changed and the Lord's Word stayed the same. We have so many people that will tell you, "My pastor said this or that," but they stop telling you what the Lord has said. Have you noticed that, or you just gotten so used to it until the Lord's Word changed? Unto the pastor's word, God said, "Let every man be a lie and my word be true." I told you that the pimps are smooth.

Let's look at another thing that you may not have thought about. The people in the church have put men on pedestals and made them their gods. That's what the prostitutes in the street do to the pimps, but we will in the church call it respect. The rain is the same in the world, just like a pimp is a pimp. Someone had to make him/her a pimp. We will pay more attention to the pimp in the pulpit than we will to God when we get to that place in our life, then we need someone to help wake us up, and that's what I am, hopefully, doing.

I hope this book will help people to, first of all, read and take their Bible to church with them. When they do go and if they do not understand, then they should pray for understanding. A person who doesn't understand is who the pimps are looking for. That's in the church and in the streets. The Word of the Lord said, "Out of all of thou getting, get an understanding." I want to tell you; do not become a target for the pimps in the pulpit or the ones in the street. We see many pastors have become a target for the pimps to bring down. Let's keep on praying for one another that we will not fall into temptation but that the Lord will deliver us from all evil. You pray for me as I pray for you.

I think that some of us forgot that we are going to leave this earth. I am not trying to plant roots here, but I am making ready to leave, and I want my sisters and my brothers to be ready to go also, but keep this one thing in mind. The Lord is coming back for His church; that's the one without a spot or any wrinkle, so in saying that, I want to be ready. I can't go back with the Lord with blood on my hand.

All pimps have blood on their hands. I would like to see the people of God start working together like they are supposed to. The Bible tells me this is how the world will know that we are Jesus's disciples, by the way that we love one another. The people in the world seem to show more love than the people in the church. We need to get back to the way of the Lord. As I think back over things, I can't help but think of how the churches operate. We will spend money building, but we won't help build people and the pastor is more concerned about how good he/she looks than they are of how the members look, but the members care about the pastors. Now take another look at how the members will give all that they have to the pastor but will not give a dime to the children or family that sits next to them in church that are in need of their help, but the pastor is getting paid from the church. What's wrong with the picture? That person was trying to buy a place with the pastor. There's so much of that going on in our church today. The pastor knows that it's going on in the church, but he/she will not stop it because of greed, and they (meaning, the pastor) know of members in the church and will not try to help that family either. Once again that's a pimp pastor preacher pimping God's people from the pulpit.

Now let me give you some news that I think that all the people in the churches need to know about some of their pimps/pastors in the pulpits. They do not have their trust in God, at least not the God that most of us serve. They have their trust in the god of black magic and witchcraft and money, and some are casting spells on people/members. This is what the Bible meant when it talked about spiritual wickedness in high places. It is in some of the largest churches in the United States, and so many of you have, and some still are, sitting under those ministries. You know they are led by witches and warlocks. The fight has already begun.

The Bible told you to know them that labored among you; some of you did, and do know who your leaders are because some of you are just like them and you see nothing wrong with it. This is what's wrong with the churches today; some pastors have sold their souls to Satan in order for them to get the big churches. This is what some have done. Those are the pimps in the pulpit, pimping God's people. Nevertheless, just do not take my word for it. Look around and ask the Lord to show you. He will show it to you if you really want to know. Keep this in mind. After this book comes out, many are going to try to stop it from going forth, but the truth will come out. You must choose the side that you will fight on. Will it be on the Lord's side, or will it be on the side of Satan? The Lord said either you are with Him or you are against Him. What about those ex-drug dealers/pimp pastors that are pimping God's people from the pulpits? There is nothing wrong with being an ex-drug dealer or anything as long as that is what it is. However, some of the so-called ex-dealers are not exes. They just bing it from the street to the pulpit. Some pastors have lied, stolen, cheated, and pimped their way to where they are now.

Oh, by the way, the people that will try to stop this book will not be the world, but it will be the ones in the church, the false preachers/pimps in the pulpits. They did Jesus the same way. I was told by a preacher that some would make up lies about me to try to stop me from the sale of this book. I told him, "Let them go ahead on." I am clean from all my past. That does not mean that I never did any wrong. I will be the first one to admit that I have done some wrong, but what are you doing now? I told him, "If you are not doing any of the things that are in this book, then don't worry about it, but if you are, then get it right with the Lord. I am not your judge in no way." In addition, I ask that all members of a church pray for your leaders that they do not become a pimp in the pulpit who is prostituting God's people.

Some pastors have turned the house of God into a country club or, then again, just a club. I hope and pray that you got an eye-opening word from this book and that it has blessed your soul with understanding. Stay on the lookout when you are in a church where you know or do not know about because it's what you don't know that can hurt you. What about that pastor that wants you to say Amen only to him/her when they are preaching? That is a pimp in the pulpit prostituting God's people.